Race

North Pole

Written by Ian Morrison
Illustrated by Spike Wademan

Arctic
NORTH POLE
NEW YORK 3,393 mi
LONDON 2,667 mi
ROME 3,380 mi
MOSCOW 2,702 mi
SOUTH POLE 12,427 mi

Contents

Who Was Robert Peary?

Robert Peary was a famous American explorer. He and his team were the first people to reach the North Pole. Peary faced many dangers along the way, but he never gave up. Many people thought that reaching the pole was impossible. Peary proved them all wrong.

1856
Robert Peary is born in Cresson, Pennsylvania.

1881
Peary joins the United States Navy.

1884
Peary travels to Central America to survey land.

1893
Peary charts the ice cap of Greenland.

Setting the Scene

The Race to the Pole

By the beginning of the 20th century, there were few places that had not been explored by Europeans. Different countries raced to be the first to reach these places.

The North Pole, the geographical point around which the Earth rotates, had never been reached by Europeans. The race to reach the North Pole was on.

1899 Peary gets frostbite and loses eight toes.

1906 Peary attempts to reach the North Pole but fails.

1909 Peary reaches the North Pole.

1920 Peary dies in Washington, D.C.

A Taste for Adventure

1881

Robert Peary loved to read. As a boy, he read books about Greenland. He became excited about this land of ice and snow. From an early age, he knew what he wanted to do with his life. In 1881, Peary joined the Navy.

Robert Peary worked hard in school. In 1877, he became a civil engineer. The United States Navy saw that his engineering skills could help them. They had a special job for him to do.

Robert Peary when he was in the United States Navy.

civil engineer a person who plans or builds things for the public to use

Going South

1884

Peary wanted to go north, but the Navy sent him south to Nicaragua, in Central America. They wanted him to search for a site for a new canal. Peary met Matthew Henson just before his second trip to Nicaragua in 1887. Henson joined Peary on this trip.

It was the beginning of a long friendship. Peary and Henson would make history together many years later.

More than once, Peary described Henson as "*the most nearly indispensable man*" and the best traveler he had ever known.

Ships had to travel a great distance to get from the Atlantic to the Pacific Ocean. The United States Navy was looking for a shorter way. They decided to build a canal to connect the two oceans. The Navy sent Peary to Nicaragua twice to look for a suitable site, but none was found.

Matthew Henson became a loyal friend to Robert Peary. He was fascinated by Arctic exploration, too. The two men shared many adventures.

Going North

1887–1906

Robert Peary took time off from the Navy. He still dreamed of finding the North Pole. He risked his life many times trying to get there. During a trip in 1899, he suffered frostbite in his feet. He had to have eight toes amputated*. This did not stop him. He was determined to keep trying until he reached his goal.*

amputate to cut off

Over the next 18 years, Peary made many trips north with Henson. They learned everything they could from the Inuit people. They became very skilled in hunting and sledding. Henson also learned the Inuit language.

Josephine Peary, Robert's wife, gave birth to their first daughter in Greenland on a trip they made in 1893–1895. They named their daughter Marie Ahnighito. The word Ahnighito is Inuit for "snow baby."

To the North Pole

1908–1909

Peary knew that he needed a special ship. The ice would crush an ordinary ship. He had already designed a special ship named the Roosevelt. *The* Roosevelt *was able to break up much of the ice in front of it. This ship had worked well on his last trip. He decided to use it again in one final attempt to reach the North Pole.*

Peary decided to make another attempt to reach the North Pole. In 1908, he left New York in the *Roosevelt*. At Greenland, many Inuit men and their families joined the crew. They sailed to Ellesmere Island in the Canadian Arctic. This was as far north as they could go by ship. Peary waited for better weather before continuing the journey.

The *Roosevelt* worked like a battering ram. It could ride up onto ice slabs and crush them with its weight.

Peary understood that crossing the frozen ocean was dangerous. He did everything possible to make the trip safe. By now, he and Henson had spent 18 years learning everything they could from the Inuit people, who have lived in the Arctic for thousands of years. Peary's team used lightweight sleds. They wore warm fur clothing made by Inuit women.

A special food called pemmican gave them energy to keep going. It was made of dried beef mixed with sugar, raisins, and suet or animal fat.

Peary was finally ready to leave Ellesmere Island. He had to cross 413 miles of ice to reach the North Pole. He set out on February 28, 1909. With him went 23 men, 19 sleds, and about 130 dogs.

The Inuit women who were aboard the *Roosevelt* (above).

Peary designed this sled and Henson built it.

A Team Approach

March 1909

The ice was dangerous. Once, Peary and his three teams were camping on an ice floe. There was a very loud noise, and the ice floe split in two!

Peary and Henson were safe on the main floe, but other men were trapped on the small piece of ice that was beginning to drift out into the open sea. They were very lucky, however. The current brought the two ice floes back together, and the men scrambled back to safety.

ice floe a sheet of floating ice

Peary used a team approach on his journey to the North Pole. There were five teams. Peary and Henson led one. Another was led by Bob Bartlett. The other three teams were led by Donald Macmillan and John Goodsell, George Borup, and Ross Marvin. The first team would make a trail and then build a camp. The second team would use the camp and then go on ahead and build the next camp.

Bob Bartlett (right) took his team to within 133 miles of the pole.

There and Back

April 1909

Peary thought hard about who would go on the final part of the journey to the pole. He chose himself, Matthew Henson, and four Inuit men, Egingwah, Oatah, Seegloo, and Ookeah.
The team was lucky. They had good weather.
The final leg of the trip took them five or six days.
On April 6, 1909, they reached the North Pole.

In his journal, Peary wrote, "*... my dream and ambition for 23 years, mine at last ...*"

The team led by Bob Bartlett set up the last camp, 133 miles from the pole. This was the farthest north anyone had ever been before. Even the Inuit, who lived in the Arctic, did not go so far north into the frozen wilderness. From there, Peary's team completed the journey.

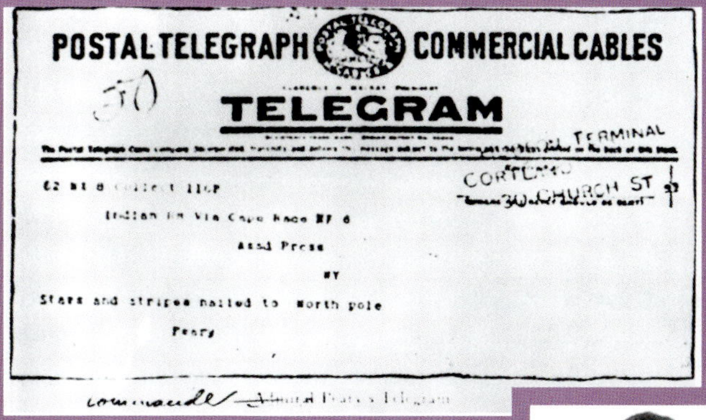
POSTAL TELEGRAPH COMMERCIAL CABLES

TELEGRAM

TERMINAL

CHURCH ST

Assd Press

NY

Stars and stripes nailed to North pole

Peary

As soon as Peary reached civilization, he announced the following message in a telegram: "Stars and stripes nailed to North Pole."

Egingwah, Oatah, Seegloo, and Ookeah

For weeks after they returned to the Roosevelt, *Peary had terrible nightmares about drowning in the cold Arctic Ocean. In real life, of course, everyone came back uninjured. Careful planning and teamwork had been the key to the success of the adventure.*

Later, Matthew Henson would write about how proud he felt to be the first African American at the North Pole.

Their adventure was not yet over. They had to travel back across more than 400 miles of dangerous ice that could shift and split without warning. They had many narrow escapes from drowning. At last they made it back to Ellesmere Island.

This picture shows Robert Peary (center) with two other famous polar explorers, Ernest Shackleton (left) and Roald Amundsen (right).

He Never Gave Up

Robert Peary searched for the North Pole for many years. Most people thought it could not be done, but Peary never gave up. Hard work and careful planning earned him success. He also had vital support from Matthew Henson, his Inuit guides, and the rest of his brave team.

Peary's achievement is still a remarkable one. Since then, many explorers who have tried to reach the North Pole have failed, even with modern technology.

Matthew Henson's headstone honors his achievement as part of the team that reached the North Pole.

Planning Was the Key

The way Robert Peary planned his trip was important to his success. Here are some of the things he did:

- He learned how to cross dangerous ice.
- He learned from the Inuit how to survive in the Arctic environment.
- He designed a special ship that could survive the journey.
- He designed sleds that are still used today.
- He used a team approach.

What If?

Some people think that Peary and his team never reached the North Pole. One person, Frederick Cook, even claimed that he had arrived there first. What if Peary's team did not reach the North Pole? Does that make their achievements less important? Why or why not?

Index

teamwork working together